Love Coupons for HER

This coupon entitles you to:

Body massage

Terms & Conditions: _____

_____

_____

This coupon entitles you to:

Breakfast in bed

Terms & Conditions: _____
_____
_____

This coupon entitles you to:

Kisses all over

Terms & Conditions: _____

_____

_____

This coupon entitles you to:

Date night

Terms & Conditions:_____

_____

_____

This coupon entitles you to:

Spa day

Terms & Conditions: _____

_____

_____

This coupon entitles you to:

Automatic victory

Terms & Conditions: _____

_____

_____

This coupon entitles you to:

69 time

Terms & Conditions: _____

_____

_____

FINAL OFFER

This coupon entitles you to:

FINAL OFFER
FINAL OFFER
FINAL OFFER

Bubble bath

Terms & Conditions: _____

_____

_____

This coupon entitles you to:

Long kiss

FINAL OFFER

Terms & Conditions: _____

_____

_____

This coupon entitles you to:

FINAL OFFER

Wild card

Terms & Conditions:_____

_____

_____

This coupon entitles you to:

Anywhere, anytime

Terms & Conditions: _____

_____

_____

This coupon entitles you to:

FINAL OFFER

Foot massage

Terms & Conditions: _____
_____
_____

This coupon entitles you to:

Cuddle Session

Terms & Conditions: _____

_____

_____

This coupon entitles you to:

FINAL OFFER

Finger fun

Terms & Conditions: _____

_____

_____

This coupon entitles you to:

Your favorite dessert

Terms & Conditions:_____

_____

_____

This coupon entitles you to:

Naked pillow fight

Terms & Conditions:_____

_____

_____

This coupon entitles you to:

FINAL OFFER
FINAL OFFER
FINAL OFFER

One whole day spent in bed

Terms & Conditions: _____
_____
_____

This coupon entitles you to:

FINAL OFFER

Free choice

Terms & Conditions: _____

_____

_____

This coupon entitles you to:

Back kisses

Terms & Conditions: _____

_____

_____

This coupon entitles you to:

FINAL OFFER

FINAL OFFER

Terms & Conditions: _____

_____

_____

This coupon entitles you to:

FINAL OFFER

FINAL OFFER

Terms & Conditions: _____

_____

_____

This coupon entitles you to:

FINAL OFFER

FINAL OFFER

Terms & Conditions: _____

_____

_____

This coupon entitles you to:

FINAL OFFER

Terms & Conditions: _____

_____

_____

This coupon entitles you to:

FINAL OFFER

Terms & Conditions:_____

_____

_____

This coupon entitles you to:

FINAL OFFER

Terms & Conditions: _____

_____

_____

This coupon entitles you to:

FINAL OFFER

Terms & Conditions: _____

_____

_____

This coupon entitles you to:

FINAL OFFER

Terms & Conditions: _____

_____

_____

This coupon entitles you to:

FINAL OFFER

Terms & Conditions:_____

_____

_____

This coupon entitles you to:

FINAL OFFER

Terms & Conditions: _____

_____

_____

This coupon entitles you to:

Terms & Conditions:_____

_____

_____

This coupon entitles you to:

FINAL OFFER

Terms & Conditions: _____

_____

_____

This coupon entitles you to:

FINAL OFFER

Terms & Conditions: _____
_____
_____

This coupon entitles you to:

FINAL OFFER

Terms & Conditions: _____

_____

_____

This coupon entitles you to:

FINAL OFFER

FINAL OFFER

Terms & Conditions: _____

_____

_____

This coupon entitles you to:

FINAL OFFER

Terms & Conditions: _____

_____

_____

This coupon entitles you to:

FINAL OFFER

Terms & Conditions:_____

_____

_____

This coupon entitles you to:

FINAL OFFER

Terms & Conditions: _____

_____

_____

This coupon entitles you to:

FINAL OFFER
FINAL OFFER

Terms & Conditions:_____

_____

_____

This coupon entitles you to:

FINAL OFFER

Terms & Conditions: _____

_____

_____

Made in the USA
Las Vegas, NV
16 January 2024

84487020R00057